This journal belongs to

........................................................................................................

Date

........................................................................................................

Trust is the basis of life. Without trust, no human being can live.

Trapeze artists offer a beautiful image of this. Flyers have to trust their catchers. They can do the most spectacular doubles, triples, or quadruples, but what finally makes their performance spectacular are the catchers who are there for them at the right time in the right place....

It is wonderful to fly in the air free as a bird, but when God isn't there to catch us, all our flying comes to nothing. Let's trust in the Great Catcher.

HENRI J. M. NOUWEN

# You are a beloved child of God.

Everything about you is precious to Him. He wants to show you the mysteries of life and give you rich blessings as you trust in Him.

We invite you to use this journal as an inspiration to "fly" with God, as Henri Nouwen says. To spend time with Him, to contemplate how much He loves you. Know that He is there to catch you. Even when other things are in question, the Catcher is not. You can trust Him with all your heart.

These pages are the place for hope words, prayer words, dream words, soaring words, try-again words. Be bold and strong in the Lord, trusting Him to let you fly but also to always draw you safely back into His arms. He will never leave you.

*The Editors*

At every moment, God is calling your name and waiting to be found.
To each cry of "Oh Lord," God answers, "I am here."

------------------------------------------------

------------------------------------------------

------------------------------------------------

------------------------------------------------

------------------------------------------------

------------------------------------------------

------------------------------------------------

------------------------------------------------

------------------------------------------------

------------------------------------------------

------------------------------------------------

------------------------------------------------

------------------------------------------------

------------------------------------------------

*God is our refuge and strength, an ever-present help in trouble.*
*Therefore we will not fear.*

PSALM 46:1–2

Heavenly Father, my prayer is that I would learn to trust You more....
May I find my strength in Your joy.

KIM BOYCE

*God has come to save me. I will trust in him and not be afraid.*
*The LORD God is my strength and my song.*

ISAIAH 12:2 NLT

When I walk by the wayside, He is along with me.... Amid all my forgetfulness of Him, He never forgets me.

THOMAS CHALMERS

*Let all that I am praise the LORD; may I never forget the good things he does for me.*

PSALM 103:2 NLT

Only God gives true peace—a quiet gift He sets within us just when we think we've exhausted our search for it.

*The Lord gives strength to his people;*
*the Lord blesses his people with peace.*

PSALM 29:11

God never abandons anyone on whom He has set His love; nor does Christ, the good shepherd, ever lose track of His sheep.

J. I. PACKER

_____

_____

_____

_____

_____

_____

_____

_____

_____

_____

_____

_____

_____

_____

_____

_____

_____

_____

*He tends his flock like a shepherd: He gathers the lambs in his*
*arms and carries them close to his heart.*

ISAIAH 40:11

Live today! Live fully each moment of today. Trust God to let you work through this moment and the next. He will give you all you need. Don't skip over the painful or confusing moment—even it has its important and rightful place in the day.

*Seek the Kingdom of God above all else, and live righteously,*
*and he will give you everything you need.*

MATTHEW 6:33 NLT

All the world is an utterance of the Almighty. Its countless beauties, its exquisite adaptations, all speak to you of Him.

PHILLIPS BROOKS

*Worship the LORD in the splendor of his holiness.*

PSALM 96:9

We are to simply trust God. While we trust, God can work.

GEORGE PARDINGTON

*The fulfillment of God's promise depends entirely on trusting God and his way, and then simply embracing him and what he does.*

ROMANS 4:16 MSG

I would rather walk with God in the dark than go alone in the light.

MARY GARDINER BRAINARD

*Yet I am always with you; you hold me by my right hand.*

PSALM 73:23

When I try, I fail. When I trust, He succeeds.

*In him our hearts rejoice, for we trust in his holy name.*
*May your unfailing love be with us, L*ORD*,*
*even as we put our hope in you.*

PSALM 33:21–22

God is within all things, but not included; outside all things,
but not excluded, above all things, but not beyond their reach.

GREGORY I

*Yours, L*ORD*, is the greatness and the power and the glory and the majesty and the splendor, for everything in heaven and earth is yours.... You are exalted as head over all.*

1 CHRONICLES 29:11

Trust [God] for the rest of the journey.
He puts the rainbow at the end of the hardest trail.

DALE EVANS ROGERS

*Your life is a journey you must travel with*
*a deep consciousness of God.*

1 Peter 1:18 msg

Lord…give me only Your love and Your grace. With this I am rich enough, and I have no more to ask.

IGNATIUS LOYOLA

_Lord, be gracious to us; we long for you. Be our strength every morning, our salvation in time of distress._

Isaiah 33:2

Therefore will I trust You always, though I may seem to be lost and in the shadow of death. I will not fear, for You are ever with me. And You will never leave me to face my perils alone.

THOMAS MERTON

.......................................................................................................

.......................................................................................................

.......................................................................................................

.......................................................................................................

.......................................................................................................

.......................................................................................................

.......................................................................................................

.......................................................................................................

.......................................................................................................

.......................................................................................................

.......................................................................................................

.......................................................................................................

.......................................................................................................

.......................................................................................................

.......................................................................................................

*Even when I walk through the darkest valley,*
*I will not be afraid, for you are close beside me.*

We walk without fear, full of hope and courage and strength to do His will,
waiting for the endless good which He is always giving as fast
as He can get us able to take it in.

GEORGE MACDONALD

*Open your mouth and taste, open your eyes and see—*
*how good GOD is. Blessed are you who run to him.*

PSALM 34:8 MSG

Lord, my hands and my heart are open to You.
I know that You are utterly trustworthy.

GLORIA GAITHER

*Trust in him at all times…pour out your hearts to him,*
*for God is our refuge.*

<small>PSALM 62:8</small>

Savor little glimpses of God's goodness and His majesty,
thankful for the gift of them.

........................................................................................................................................

........................................................................................................................................

........................................................................................................................................

........................................................................................................................................

........................................................................................................................................

........................................................................................................................................

........................................................................................................................................

........................................................................................................................................

........................................................................................................................................

........................................................................................................................................

........................................................................................................................................

........................................................................................................................................

........................................................................................................................................

........................................................................................................................................

........................................................................................................................................

........................................................................................................................................

........................................................................................................................................

........................................................................................................................................

*LORD, our Lord, how majestic is your name in all the earth!*
*You have set your glory in the heavens.*

PSALM 8:1

> For God's love is literally infinite. It is the shoreless sea we are destined to swim in, surf in, and grow in forever.
>
> PETER KREEFT

*God's love…is ever and always,*
*eternally present to all who fear him.*

PSALM 103:17 MSG

God still draws near to us in the ordinary, commonplace, everyday
experiences and places.... He comes in surprising ways.

HENRY GARIEPY

_I have set the LORD always before me: because he is at my right hand,_
_I shall not be moved._

PSALM 16:8 KJV

Abandon yourself to His care and guidance, as a sheep in the care of a shepherd, and trust Him utterly.

HANNAH WHITALL SMITH

---

---

---

---

---

---

---

---

---

---

---

---

---

---

---

---

---

---

---

---

---

*The LORD is my shepherd, I have all that I need.*

PSALM 23:1 NLT

Whatever the circumstances, whatever the call...His strength will be your
strength in your hour of need.

BILLY GRAHAM

........................................................................................................................................................
........................................................................................................................................................
........................................................................................................................................................
........................................................................................................................................................
........................................................................................................................................................
........................................................................................................................................................
........................................................................................................................................................
........................................................................................................................................................
........................................................................................................................................................
........................................................................................................................................................
........................................................................................................................................................
........................................................................................................................................................
........................................................................................................................................................
........................................................................................................................................................
........................................................................................................................................................
........................................................................................................................................................
........................................................................................................................................................
........................................................................................................................................................
........................................................................................................................................................
........................................................................................................................................................
........................................................................................................................................................
........................................................................................................................................................

*Ah, Sovereign Lord, you have made the heavens
and the earth by your great power and outstretched arm.
Nothing is too hard for you.*

JEREMIAH 32:17

The best proof of love is trust.

DR. JOYCE BROTHERS

*Let the morning bring me word of your unfailing love,*
*for I have put my trust in you. Show me the way I should go,*
*for to you I entrust my life.*

PSALM 143:8

Live for today but hold your hands open to tomorrow. Anticipate the future and its changes with joy. There is a seed of God's love in every event, every circumstance, every unpleasant situation in which you may find yourself.

BARBARA JOHNSON

_The joy of the L_ORD _is your strength._

NEHEMIAH 8:10 KJV

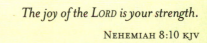

When we commit a predicament, a possibility, a person to God in genuine confidence, we do not merely step aside and tap our foot until God comes through…. We remain in contact with God in gratitude and praise.

EUGENIA PRICE

*Give thanks to the LORD, for he is good!*
*His faithful love endures forever.*

1 CHRONICLES 16:34 NLT

You will trust God only as much as you love Him. And you will love Him not because you have studied Him; you will love Him because you have touched Him—in response to His touch.

BRENNAN MANNING

---
---
---
---
---
---
---
---
---
---
---
---
---
---
---

*The LORD is gracious and full of compassion, slow to anger
and great in mercy. The LORD is good to all,
and His tender mercies are over all His works.*

PSALM 145:8–9 NKJV

I think of faith as a kind of whistling in the dark because, in much the same way, it helps to give us courage and to hold the shadows at bay. To whistle in the dark...demonstrate[s], if only to ourselves, that not even the dark can quite overcome our trust in the ultimate triumph of the Living Light.

FREDERICK BUECHNER

*For You light my lamp; the LORD my God illumines my darkness.*

PSALM 18:28 NASB

Faith sees the invisible, believes the incredible, and receives the impossible.

*With God all things are possible.*

MARK 10:27 KJV

You can trust God right now to supply all your needs for today.
And if your needs are more tomorrow, His supply will be greater also.

*God will supply all your needs according to his riches in glory.*

PHILIPPIANS 4:19 NASB

A life transformed by the power of God is always a marvel and a miracle.

GERALDINE NICHOLAS

_____

_____

_____

_____

_____

_____

_____

_____

_____

_____

_____

_____

_____

_____

_____

_____

_____

_Create in me a clean heart, O God;_
_and renew a right spirit within me._

Trust! The way will open, the right issue will come, the end will be peace, the cloud will be lifted, and the light of eternal noonday shall shine at last.

L. B. COWMAN

*The LORD is my light and my salvation; whom shall I fear?*
*The LORD is the strength of my life; of whom shall I be afraid?*

PSALM 27:1 NKJV

Grace means that God already loves us as much as
an infinite God can possibly love.

PHILIP YANCEY

*By grace you have been saved through faith;
and that not of yourselves, it is the gift of God.*

EPHESIANS 2:8 NASB

Anxiety is the rust of life, destroying its brightness and weakening its power. A childlike and abiding trust in [God] is its best [prevention] and remedy.

HORACE BUSHNELL

*O Lord, you alone are my hope. I've trusted you,*
*O Lord, from childhood.*

PSALM 71:5 NLT

Be still, and in the quiet moments, listen to the voice of
your heavenly Father. His words can renew your spirit.
No one knows you and your needs like He does.

JANET L. SMITH

*You're my place of quiet retreat; I wait for your Word to renew me....*
*Therefore I lovingly embrace everything you say.*

PSALM 119:114, 119 MSG

God never violates the trust we put in Him.

NEVA COYLE

_You who live in the shelter of the Most High, who abide in the shadow_
_of the Almighty, will say to the Lord, "My refuge and my fortress;_
_my God, in whom I trust."_

PSALM 91:1–2 NRSV

Look deep within yourself and recognize what brings life and grace into your heart. It is this that can be shared with those around you. You are loved by God. This is an inspiration to love.

CHRISTOPHER DE VINCK

*Your love, Lord, reaches to the heavens, your faithfulness
to the skies.... How priceless is your unfailing love.*

PSALM 36:5, 7 NIV

Lord, grant me a quiet mind,
That trusting You, for You are kind,
I may go on without a fear,
For You, my Lord, are always near.

AMY CARMICHAEL

*In quietness and trust is your strength.*

ISAIAH 30:15

The Lord promises to bind up the brokenhearted, to give relief and full
deliverance to those whose spirits have been weighed down.

CHARLES R. SWINDOLL

_The LORD is close to the brokenhearted and saves_
_those who are crushed in spirit._

PSALM 34:18

What is the Lord saying? There's only one message: "Trust Me. Even when you don't understand and can't comprehend: trust Me!"

DR. JAMES DOBSON

*Trust in the Lord with all your heart and lean not
on your own understanding; in all your ways submit
to him, and he will make your paths straight.*

<small>Proverbs 3:5–6</small>

The reason for loving God is God Himself, and the measure in which
we should love Him is to love Him without measure.

BERNARD OF CLAIRVAUX

*Love the LORD your God with all your heart,*
*all your soul, and all your strength.*

DEUTERONOMY 6:5 NLT

If we have been learning to worship God and to trust Him,
the crisis will reveal that we will go to the breaking point
and not break in our confidence in Him.

OSWALD CHAMBERS

*I trust in the LORD. I will be glad and rejoice in your*
*unfailing love, for you have seen my troubles,*
*and you care about the anguish of my soul.*

PSALM 31:6–7 NLT

Just when we least expect it, [God] intrudes into our neat and tidy notions
about who He is and how He works.

JONI EARECKSON TADA

*"My thoughts are nothing like your thoughts," says the Lord.*
*"And my ways are far beyond anything you could imagine."*

Isaiah 55:8 nlt

When you have nothing left but God...you become aware that God is enough.

A. MAUDE ROYDEN

*LORD, you alone are my portion and my cup;*
*you make my lot secure.*

Know by the light of faith that God is present,
and be content with directing all your actions toward Him.

BROTHER LAWRENCE

*If I rise on the wings of the dawn, if I settle*
*on the far side of the sea, even there your hand will guide me,*
*your right hand will hold me fast.*

PSALM 139:9–10

When we have hope, we are showing that we
trust God to work out the situation.

BARBARA JOHNSON

*May the God of hope fill you with all joy and peace*
*as you trust in him, so that you may overflow*
*with hope by the power of the Holy Spirit.*

ROMANS 15:13

Trust the past to the mercy of God, the present to His love,
and the future to His providence.

AUGUSTINE

*Do not worry then, saying, "What will we eat?" or "What will we drink?" or "What will we wear for clothing?" ...Your heavenly Father knows that you need all these things.*

MATTHEW 6:31–32 NASB

We shall steer safely through every storm, so long as our heart is right,
our intention fervent, our courage steadfast, and our trust fixed on God.

FRANCIS DE SALES

*You will keep in perfect peace those whose minds are steadfast,*
*because they trust in you.*

ISAIAH 26:3

You are...infinitely dear to the Father,
unspeakably precious to Him. You are never, not for one second, alone.

NORMAN DOWTY

*My Presence will go with you, and I will give you rest.*

EXODUS 33:14

There is no unbelief;
Whoever plants a seed beneath the sod
And waits to see it push away the clod,
He trusts in God.

ELIZABETH YORK

*Neither the one who plants nor the one who waters is anything,*
*but God who causes the growth.*

1 Corinthians 3:7 nasb

We may...depend upon God's promises, for...He will be as good as His word.

MATTHEW HENRY

*Not one word of all the good words which the LORD your God spoke concerning you has failed; all have been fulfilled for you, not one of them has failed.*

JOSHUA 23:14 NASB

Father, help me to see the dark threads, too, as part of Your design.
And so learn to trust You in all things.

ELIZABETH SHERRILL

*Do not let your hearts be troubled. You believe in God.*

JOHN 14:1

There is nothing but God's grace. We walk upon it; we breathe it;
we live and die by it; it makes the nails and axles of the universe.

ROBERT LOUIS STEVENSON

*God is sheer mercy and grace; not easily angered,*
*he's rich in love…. As far as sunrise is from sunset,*
*he has separated us from our sins.*

PSALM 103:8, 12 MSG

When we trust as far as we can, we often find ourselves
able to trust at least a little further.

MARK GIBBARD

........................................................................................................

........................................................................................................

........................................................................................................

........................................................................................................

........................................................................................................

........................................................................................................

........................................................................................................

........................................................................................................

........................................................................................................

........................................................................................................

........................................................................................................

........................................................................................................

........................................................................................................

........................................................................................................

........................................................................................................

........................................................................................................

........................................................................................................

*We stopped relying on ourselves and learned to rely only on God.*

2 Corinthians 1:9 nlt

Leave behind your fear and focus on the lovingkindness of God
so that you may recover by looking at Him.

_One thing I ask from the L_ORD_...that I may dwell in the house of the L_ORD _all the days of my life, to gaze on the beauty of the L_ORD_._

PSALM 27:4

God is here. I have joyously discovered that He is always
up to something in my life, and I am learning to quit
second-guessing Him and simply trust the process.

GLORIA GAITHER

*I know the one in whom I trust, and I am sure that he
is able to guard what I have entrusted to him.*

2 TIMOTHY 1:12 NLT

Retire from the world each day to some private spot.... Listen for the inward Voice till you learn to recognize it.... Learn to pray inwardly every moment.

A. W. TOZER

*I pray that out of his glorious riches he may strengthen you*
*with power through his Spirit in your inner being.*

EPHESIANS 3:16

The grace is God's: the faith is ours. God gave us the free will with which to choose. God gave us the capacity to believe and trust.

BILLY GRAHAM

*Have faith in God. I tell you the truth, you can say to this mountain, "May you be lifted up and thrown into the sea," and it will happen. But you must really believe it.*

MARK 11:22–23 NLT

Heaven often seems distant and unknown, but if He who made the road…
is our guide, we need not fear to lose the way.

HENRY VAN DYKE

*I'll be right there to show them what roads to take, make sure
they don't fall into the ditch. These are the things I'll be doing for them—
sticking with them, not leaving them for a minute.*

ISAIAH 42:16 MSG

They that trust the Lord find many things to praise Him for.
Praise follows trust.

LILY MAY

*The LORD is my strength and my shield; my heart
trusts in him, and he helps me. My heart leaps
for joy, and with my song I praise him.*

PSALM 28:7

Do not be afraid to enter the cloud that is settling down on your life.
God is in it. The other side is radiant with His glory.

L. B. COWMAN

*His way is in the whirlwind and the storm,*
*and clouds are the dust of his feet.*

Nahum 1:3

Calmly, quietly, trust in God. Relax and let God take full control.
Yes, quietly trust.

THELMA McMILLAN

*The Lord your God in your midst…. He will quiet you
with His love, He will rejoice over you with singing.*

ZEPHANIAH 3:17 NKJV

Genuine love sees faces, not a mass:
the Good Shepherd calls His own sheep by name.

GEORGE A. BUTTRICK

*Do not be afraid, for I have ransomed you.*
*I have called you by name; you are mine.*

ISAIAH 43:1 NLT

Let us shut our eyes...to that which God hides from us.
Let us worship without seeing.

FRANÇOIS FÉNELON

........................................................................

........................................................................

........................................................................

........................................................................

........................................................................

........................................................................

........................................................................

........................................................................

........................................................................

........................................................................

........................................................................

........................................................................

........................................................................

*The secret things belong to the L*ORD *our God,*
*but the things revealed belong to us...forever, that we*
*may follow all the words of this law.*

DEUTERONOMY 29:29

We need more than a watchmaker who winds up the universe and lets it tick.
We need love and mercy and forgiveness and grace—
qualities only a personal God can offer.

PHILIP YANCEY

*The LORD will personally go ahead of you. He will be with you;*
*he will neither fail you nor abandon you.*

DEUTERONOMY 31:8 NLT

Thank You, Lord, for this chance to stretch some more in Your direction—
to trust You when I cannot understand.

Quin Sherrer

*Trials will show that your faith is genuine. It is being
tested as fire tests and purifies gold—though your
faith is far more precious than mere gold.*

1 Peter 1:7 nlt

God, who is love—who is, if I may say it this way, made out of love—
simply cannot help but shed blessing on blessing upon us.

HANNAH WHITALL SMITH

*The Lord bless you and keep you; the Lord make His face shine on you and be gracious to you; the Lord turn his face toward you and give you peace.*

Numbers 6:24–26

God's timing is rarely our timing. But far better than we do, He numbers our days and knows our moments and our hours. Our task is to trust.

Os Guinness

*Blessed is the one who trusts in the LORD.*

PROVERBS 16:20

God, who has led you safely on so far, will lead you on to the end.
Be altogether at rest…in His heavenly providence.

FRANCIS DE SALES

_The peace of God, which surpasses all understanding,
will guard your hearts and minds._

PHILIPPIANS 4:7 NKJV

Trust Him when dark doubts assail you
Trust Him when your strength is small,
Trust Him when to simply trust Him
Seems the hardest thing of all.

SALESIAN MISSIONS

*Those who hope in the LORD will renew their strength.*
*They will soar on wings like eagles; they will run*
*and not grow weary, they will walk and not be faint.*

ISAIAH 40:31

When God has become…our refuge and our fortress, then we can reach out
to Him in the midst of a broken world and feel at home while still on the way.

HENRI J. M. NOUWEN

*Hear my cry, O God.... For You have been a refuge for me,*
*a tower of strength against the enemy. Let me dwell in Your tent*
*forever; let me take refuge in the shelter of Your wings.*

PSALM 61:1, 3–4 NASB

Praise [God] for all that is past. Trust Him for all that is to come.

JOSEPH HART

When I am afraid, I put my trust in you. In God,
whose word I praise—in God I trust and am not afraid.

PSALM 56:3–4

God is with us in the midst of our daily, routine lives. In the middle of cleaning the house or driving somewhere in the pickup…. Often it's in the middle of the most mundane task that He lets us know He is there with us.

MICHAEL CARD

*Because* G<small>OD</small> *will be right there with you;*
*he'll keep you safe and sound.*

P<small>ROVERBS</small> 3:26 <small>MSG</small>

Knowing God is putting your trust in Him. Trust that He loves you
and will provide for your every need.

TOM RICHARDS

*God will generously provide all you need.*

2 CORINTHIANS 9:8 NLT

An instant of pure love is more precious to God...
than all other good works together.

JOHN OF THE CROSS

*Love never gives up, never loses faith, is always hopeful,*
*and endures through every circumstance.*

1 CORINTHIANS 13:7 NLT

The way may at times seem dark, but light will arise,
if you trust in the Lord, and wait patiently for Him.

ELIZABETH T. KING

*Be still before the L*ORD *and wait patiently for him.*

PSALM 37:7

When God finds a soul that rests in Him and is not easily moved...
to this same soul He gives the joy of His presence.

CATHERINE OF GENOA

*You make known to me the path of life; you will fill me with joy in your presence, with eternal pleasures at your right hand.*

PSALM 16:11

God will never, never, never let us down if we have faith
and put our trust in Him. He will always look after us.

MOTHER TERESA

_Those who know your name trust in you, for you, LORD,
have never forsaken those who seek you._

PSALM 9:10

Open wide the windows of our spirits and fill us full of light;
open wide the door of our hearts, that we may receive and entertain
You with all our powers of adoration.

CHRISTINA ROSSETTI

*You give [us] drink from your river of delights. For with you is the fountain of life; in your light we see light.*

PSALM 36:8-9

Our faith…is not based upon our ability to conjure up some special feeling.
Rather, it is built upon a confident assurance in the faithfulness of God.
We focus on His trustworthiness and especially on His steadfast love.

RICHARD J. FOSTER

*The faithful love of the L*ORD *never ends!*
*His mercies never cease.*
*Great is his faithfulness.*

LAMENTATIONS 3:22–23 NLT

Ellie Claire™ Gift & Paper Corp.
Minneapolis, MN 55378
EllieClaire.com

*Trust in the Lord with All Your Heart*
© 2013 Ellie Claire Gift & Paper Corp.

ISBN 978-1-60936-917-0

Compiled by Marilyn Jansen
Cover and interior design by Gearbox | studiogearbox.com
Typesetting by Jeff Jansen | aestheticsoup.net

Printed in China